Project

Space

THE PROJECT MAKERS

Ian Graham

WINDMILL BOOKS

Published in 2020 by Windmill Books,
an imprint of Rosen Publishing
29 East 21ˢᵗ Street, New York, NY 10010

Copyright © 2020 Miles Kelly Publishing

Publishing Director: Belinda Gallagher
Creative Director: Jo Cowan
Senior Editor: Sarah Parkin
Designer: Joe Jones
Consultant: Clint Twist
Indexer: Jane Parker
Image Manager: Liberty Newton
Production: Elizabeth Collins, Caroline Kelly
Reprographics: Stephan Davis, Thom Allaway
Assets: Lorraine King

Cataloging-in-Publication Data

Names: Graham, Ian.
Title: Project space / Ian Graham.
Description: New York : Windmill Books, 2020.
| Series: The project makers | Includes index.
Identifiers: ISBN 9781538392379 (pbk.) | ISBN 9781725393073 (library bound)
| ISBN 9781538392386 (6 pack)
Subjects: LCSH: Astronomy--Juvenile literature.
| Solar system--Juvenile literature. | Handicraft--Juvenile literature.
Classification: LCC QB46.G724 2019 | DDC 520--dc23
Manufactured in the United States of America

CPSIA Compliance Information:
Batch #BW20WM:
For Further Information
contact Rosen Publishing,
New York, New York
at 1-800-237-9932

How to use the projects

This book is packed full of amazing facts about space. There are also 11 cool projects, designed to make the subject come alive.

Before you start a project:

• Read the instructions carefully and ask an adult if you need help.

• Gather all the supplies you need.

• Clear a surface to work on and cover it with newspaper.

• Wear an apron or old T-shirt to protect your clothing.

Notes for helpers:

• Children will need supervision for the projects, usually because they require the use of scissors, or preparation beforehand.

• Read the instructions together before starting and help to gather the equipment.

SAFETY FIRST!
Be careful when using glue or anything sharp, such as scissors.

IMPORTANT NOTICE
The publisher and author cannot be held responsible for any injuries, damage, or loss resulting from the use or misuse of any of the information in this book.

How to use:
If your project doesn't work the first time, try again — just have fun!

Warning:
If the project has a warning, make sure you read it carefully.

WARNING:
Never look at the Sun, especially with binoculars or a telescope. This can seriously damage your eyes or even make you blind.

Eclipse kit

To see how an eclipse works, you can make this model. You will need to ask an adult for help.

SUPPLIES

shoebox • scissors • black card stock •
• yellow tissue paper • tape • toothpicks

HOW TO MAKE

1. Cut a window at each end of your shoebox and then cut a slit across the top of the box.

2. Cut out a square of black card stock small enough to slide into the slit in the box.

3. Cut a circle out of the middle of the card stock; stick yellow tissue paper over the hole.

4. Stick a toothpick to the black card stock circle (you will use this as your Moon).

5. Slide the square of card stock into the slit in the box and hold the box up to the light. Look through it to see your Sun.

Supplies:
The equipment should be easy to find, around the house or from a craft store. Always ask before using materials from home.

Numbered stages:
Each stage of the project is numbered and illustrated. Follow the stages in the order shown to complete the project. If glue or paint is used, make sure it is dry before moving on to the next stage.

HOW TO USE
Push your Moon into the slit in the box behind the square of card stock. Move it slowly across your Sun to make an eclipse.

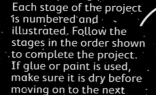

CONTENTS

WHAT IS SPACE?

When you look up into the clear, dark sky after the Sun has gone down, you're looking at space. Space is the blackness of the night sky — the vast gaps between the stars and planets — and there's lots of it!

IS SPACE EMPTY?

Space looks as if it is completely empty, but it isn't empty at all. Particles of gas and grains of dust whiz about in space all the time, but they're so small and spread out so thinly that you can't see them. Even astronauts in space can't see them.

A telescope looks out into space from a mountaintop above the clouds on the island of La Palma in the Canary Islands.

If you could drive a car straight upward, you could reach **space** in **less** than an **hour!**

WHAT CAN YOU SEE IN SPACE?

The biggest, brightest thing in the night sky is the Moon. It travels through space with Earth. The two worlds are 238,855 miles (384,400 km) apart. They're held together by an invisible force called gravity, which also holds you down on the ground!

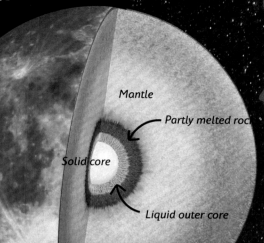

Mantle

Partly melted rock

Solid core

Liquid outer core

Where does space begin?

Space isn't very far away. It begins about 62 miles (100 km) above your head. At this height, there is almost no air at all.

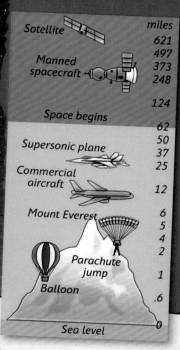

	miles
Satellite	621
	497
Manned spacecraft	373
	248
	124
Space begins	62
	50
Supersonic plane	37
	25
Commercial aircraft	12
Mount Everest	6
	5
	4
	2
Parachute jump	1
Balloon	.6
Sea level	0

Paper moon

You can make your own moon from a balloon and strips of newspaper.

SUPPLIES

newspaper • round balloon • PVA glue • bowl • water-based black and white paint • paintbrush

HOW TO MAKE

1. Tear the newspaper into strips.

2. Blow up the balloon until it is a small, round shape and tie a knot in its neck.

3. Put some PVA glue into a bowl.

4. Dip a strip of newspaper into the glue and lay it on the balloon. Add more glued strips, overlapping them until the whole balloon is covered. Build up thicker layers in some places to make mountains.

5. When the glue is dry, you can paint your moon. Mix the black and white paint to make shades of gray. Add shadowy craters just like the real Moon.

HOW TO USE

Look at your moon and see how it compares to the real thing.

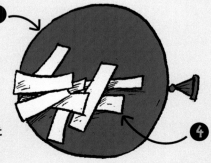
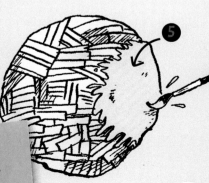

BIG BANG

Where do the stars and planets come from? Scientists think that everything was once a tiny speck, thousands of times smaller than a pinhead! The speck burst out in a huge explosion called the Big Bang. It was the birth of everything.

The first atoms

The first particles

2
A fraction of a second after the Big Bang, the universe cooled down enough for some of its energy to change into the first particles.

1
The universe created by the Big Bang was a superhot fireball. It started small, but grew bigger, and it cooled as it grew.

3
After three more minutes, the universe had cooled to less than one billion degrees Fahrenheit — cool enough for the particles to start joining together, forming more complex particles.

LIFE ON EARTH
About 3,500 million years ago (mya), or about one billion years after Earth formed, life appeared on Earth.

TIMELINE

Earth formed
4,600 mya

First life on Earth 3,500 mya
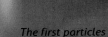

Fish 500 mya

Land plants
475 mya

Insects
400 mya

STILL GROWING

The universe has been growing bigger ever since the Big Bang. It's still growing today. Scientists can see distant parts of the universe rushing away from us. It will keep on growing for a long time. No one knows if it will ever stop growing.

The first stars

6 As the first stars came and went, they spread gas and dust through space. This formed the stars and planets we see today.

The planets we see today

Puffed-up universe

4 When the universe was 300,000 years old, it had cooled enough for the first atoms to form. Atoms are the building blocks of everything you can see.

5 The universe was filled with clouds of gas, mostly hydrogen and helium. One billion years after the Big Bang, gravity started pulling clumps of gas together — they became the first stars.

You can see how the expanding universe makes everything move further apart by making your own from a balloon.

SUPPLIES
round balloon • black permanent marker • ruler

HOW TO MAKE
1. Draw two black dots on the balloon. Use the ruler to space them about one centimeter apart.
2. Blow up the balloon and tie a knot in its neck.

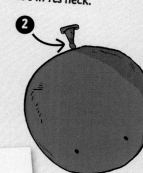

Long ago, people thought the **Universe** was powered by a giant **machine!**

More complex atoms

HOW TO USE
Measure how far apart the dots are. They are now further than one centimeter apart. As the universe expands, parts of it move further apart.

The first simple living things developed into more complex plants and animals, but it took billions of years. Single living cells joined together to make all sorts of different plants and animals.

Reptiles 300 mya

Mammals 200 mya

Birds 150 mya

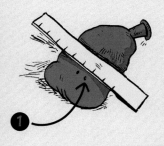

Dinosaurs die out 65 mya

Modern humans 200,000 years ago

SUPER SIZZLERS

The night sky is full of thousands of stars. The Sun is a star. Some stars are bigger than our Sun, others are smaller. They look like tiny points of light because they are much farther away from us than our Sun.

STAR BRIGHT

Why do you think stars are so bright? They look as if they're burning, but they don't burn like a flame. Stars are more like nuclear power stations in space. Their heat and light come from particles of matter smashing into each other in the center of each star. This is called nuclear fusion.

The Pleiades cluster is a group of hot blue stars. The haze around them is dust lit up by the stars.

When the Sun turns into a red giant, it might grow big enough to **swallow** the Earth, but not for another **five billion** years!

munch munch

RED GIANT

When a star forms (1) it shines brightly. A star like the Sun shines for billions of years (2). When it runs out of fuel, it swells up and cools down (3). As it cools, it becomes a red giant star (4). Then it pushes most of its gas away into space, leaving a tiny fading star called a white dwarf (5).

GOING TO PIECES

When stars bigger than the Sun grow into red giants, they blow themselves to bits in a cosmic explosion called a supernova. This sends all the elements made by the star flying out into space. The center of the star collapses and forms a strange dark star, called a neutron star.

Black hole

The universe is everything that exists everywhere. How long ago do you think the Big Bang started it all off?

Cool stars

Stars are different **colors**. Scientists can tell how hot a star is from its color. The **Sun** is a yellow star.

Hottest

Blue star

White star

Yellow star

Orange star

Red star

Coolest

Twinkle, twinkle, little star

Stars twinkle because starlight bends and twists as it travels through the air around Earth. You can see this happening by making your own stars and making them twinkle.

SUPPLIES

glass bowl • cardboard (from a cereal box) • scissors • pen • aluminium foil • flashlight

HOW TO MAKE

1. Pour cold water into the bowl until it's about two-thirds full.

2. Cut out a piece of cardboard bigger than the base of the bowl.

3. Draw small star shapes on the aluminium foil. Cut them out.

4. Place the stars on top of the cardboard and then place the bowl on top of the stars.

HOW TO USE

Close the curtains to darken the room and switch on the flashlight. Point it down into the bowl. Now tap the bowl and see the stars twinkle. The light from the flashlight is bent as it passes through the rippling water, in the same way as starlight is bent as it passes through the air around Earth.

STAR CITIES

Stars travel through space with other stars. They huddle together in galaxies. Each galaxy has billions of stars and there are billions of galaxies. Most galaxies are so far away that you need a telescope to see them.

Elliptical galaxy

Too Cool!

The biggest galaxies have one **trillion** (1,000 billion) stars.

Elliptical galaxies are the shape of a ball, or a ball that's been squashed. Some have such a squashed shape that they look long and thin.

Irregular galaxies have all sorts of different shapes. They may have been formed by collisions and near misses between different galaxies.

Stars and **galaxies** are so far apart that the distances between them are measured in **light-years**. A light-year is the distance light travels in a year.

The smallest galaxies have fewer than one **billion** (1,000 million) stars.

Irregular galaxy

Spiral galaxy

Spiral galaxies have long arms of stars curling out from a big ball of stars at the center. About three-quarters of all galaxies are spirals.

CRASH COURSE

It can take billions of years, but galaxies sometimes crash into each other. When two galaxies meet, long streams of stars are sent flying away. The two galaxies might stay together to form a new galaxy, or part and go their separate ways.

These colliding galaxies are called the Mice Galaxies because of their long tails of stars.

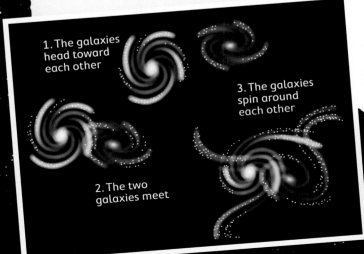

1. The galaxies head toward each other

2. The two galaxies meet

3. The galaxies spin around each other

Galactic art

Galaxies travel through space together in groups. We travel in a group of about 50 galaxies. Make your own group of galaxies!

SUPPLIES

plastic sheet (or trash bag) • coffee filters • water-based markers • eyedropper (or drinking straw) • cup of water • glue stick • glitter • scissors • large sheet of black paper

HOW TO MAKE

1. Lay the plastic sheet on the floor or a table and place the coffee filters on top of it.

2. Use the water-based markers to draw galaxies of stars on the coffee filters. Draw spirals, ellipses (squashed circles), and odd shapes, and make them different sizes.

3. Use the eyedropper to drip water from the cup onto the coffee filters, making the colors run together. Leave the filters to dry.

4. Spread glue over your galaxies and sprinkle glitter on top. Leave to dry, then cut them out. Stick your galaxies to the black paper.

HOW TO USE

Display your colorful group-of-galaxies poster on your wall.

GAS AND DUST

Stars aren't the only things in galaxies. There are clouds of gas and dust, too, called nebulae. Some of this gas and dust is all that remains of old stars. The matter you are made of came from stars, too — you are made of stardust!

COOL!

LIGHT AND DARK

Some nebulae glow because they are heated or lit up by nearby stars. Hot hydrogen gas in a nebula glows pink. Starlight reflected by a nebula looks blue. Some parts of a nebula are as dark as night, because thick dust blocks the light from glowing stars and gas behind them.

New stars are forming inside these vast pillars of gas and dust in the Eagle Nebula.

HOT AND COLD

The Boomerang Nebula is the coldest place in the universe — a teeth-chattering –521.6°F (–272°C). The Tarantula Nebula is one of the hottest — stars heat it to more than one million degrees.

The Boomerang Nebula is made of gas rushing away from a central star.

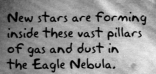

COSMIC CRAB

Some nebulae are made by exploding stars. The explosion throws gas and dust out in all directions. The Crab Nebula was caused by a star that exploded nearly 1,000 years ago. Someone looked at it through a telescope and thought it looked like a crab!

Star nurseries

Stars are born in **nebulae**. It takes about ten million years to make a star.

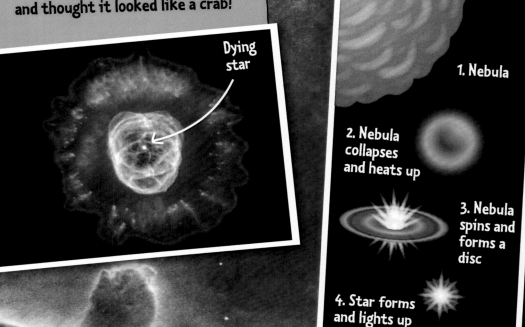

Dying star

1. Nebula

2. Nebula collapses and heats up

3. Nebula spins and forms a disc

4. Star forms and lights up

Looking for nebulae

Some nebulae are big enough and bright enough to see without a telescope. You just have to know where to look.

WHAT TO DO

Look for the constellation (group of stars) called Orion. If you live in the northern half of Earth, Orion appears in the night sky during the autumn and winter. If you live in the southern half of Earth, it appears in the spring and summer. It looks like this.

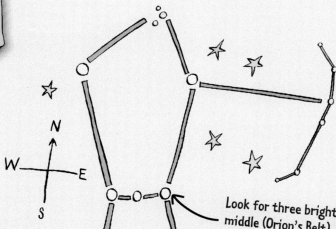

N
W — E
S

Look for three bright stars across the middle (Orion's Belt). If you live in the northern half of Earth, look down until you come to something that looks like a fuzzy star. It isn't a star at all — it's the Orion Nebula. If you live in the southern half of Earth, you'll see Orion the other way up.

GREEDY GALAXY

The galaxy we live in is called the Milky Way. It's a spiral galaxy, with arms of stars and nebulae curling out from a bulging center. It is thought that the Milky Way may have built itself up by swallowing other, smaller galaxies.

Too Cool!

The Milky Way formed about **12 billion** years ago, just 1-2 billion years after the **Big Bang**

The Milky Way moves through space at the incredible speed of **1.4 million** miles (2.2 million km) per hour!

Our galaxy is spinning. The Sun makes one lap every **230** million years!

1 If aliens from a faraway galaxy arrived at the edge of the Milky Way, they would find a vast disc of stars and dust clouds.

2 Moving toward the center of the galaxy, the aliens would travel through arms of stars in the shape of a flattened disc.

3 As the aliens neared the center of the Milky Way, they would find a big bulging ball of stars. These are mainly older stars.

6

Scientists think a gigantic, matter-gobbling black hole is at the center of the Milky Way. The aliens might have to be careful to avoid being sucked in!

5

The bulge of stars hides the center of the galaxy. What do you think the aliens will find when they get there?

4

As the aliens circled the galaxy, they might notice a star with eight planets going around it — our solar system.

PATHWAY IN THE SKY

The dusty, gassy spiral arms of our galaxy look like a hazy band of light stretching across the night sky. People in the ancient world didn't know what this strange sight was, but their myths and legends tried to explain it. The ancient Greeks thought it was a trail of milk spilled by the goddes Hera.

If you look up into a clear sky in a very dark place, especially between June and September, you might see the Milky Way.

THE SUN'S FAMILY

The solar system is made up of the eight planets, their moons, and all the smaller objects that circle the Sun. Some of the planets are small and rocky, others are huge and gassy — but they are all part of Earth's family in space.

WOWZERS!

If you were a space traveler, you would see awesome features to write home about.

The enormous extinct volcano, Olympus Mons, on Mars is a must-see. It's three times taller than Mount Everest — the tallest mountain on Earth!

It takes a spacecraft at least five months to reach Sun-scorched Mercury from Earth, but the sight of its crater-scarred surface is worth the journey.

The Moon

Venus

Mercury

Earth

Mars

You are here!

If the Sun was the size of a **bowling ball**, the solar system would be just **.99 mile** (1.6 km) across!

Venus's choking atmosphere hides its surface from view, so you have to go below the clouds to see its hostile landscape of volcanoes, valleys, and weird lava formations.

Wandering planets

The planets in the solar system seem to wander around the sky. They orbit the Sun at different speeds. Earth travels through space on its endless journey around the Sun more than twice as fast as Jupiter and nearly six times faster than Neptune.

The ancient Greeks came up with the word "planet", meaning wanderer, for these objects, which they thought looked like wandering stars in the sky.

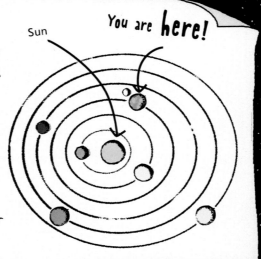

Sun

You are here!

Asteroid belt

Jupiter

Millions of weird-shaped rocks called **asteroids** can be found between Mars and Jupiter.

Jupiter's biggest moons

Ganymede is the Solar System's **largest moon** and is **bigger** than Mercury.

Jupiter's four biggest moons are called the Galilean moons, because they were discovered in 1610 by the Italian astronomer Galileo Galilei.

Io

Europa

Ganymede

Callisto

If there was a **bathtub** big enough to hold **Saturn**, it would float in the water!

The incredible ice geysers on Saturn's moon, Enceladus, are rare in the solar system. No expedition to the planets would be complete without a snapshot!

Uranus's biggest moons

Saturn

Saturn's biggest moons

How many moons?
Generally, the bigger the planet, the more moons it has. Jupiter, the biggest planet, with the strongest gravity, has the most.

Mercury	Venus	Earth	Mars	Jupiter	Saturn	Uranus	Neptune
0	0	1	2	64	62	27	13

Neptune's gassy surface is streaked with raging storms and bands of clouds. Its freezing conditions make it a desolate place, so you won't want to linger for long.

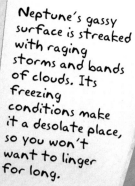

Uranus

Heat and pressure inside **Neptune** change methane gas into **diamonds!**

Neptune

Neptune's biggest moons

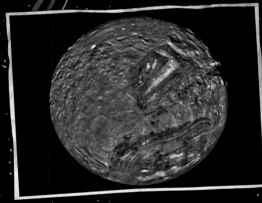

One of Uranus's moons, Miranda, has a fascinating surface, with giant canyons as much as 12 times as deep as the Grand Canyon on Earth!

Uranus rolls around on its side, giving it weird seasons. Each pole has 42 years of continuous **daylight,** then 42 years of **night!**

Cool planets

Planets closer to the **Sun,** such as Mercury and Venus, are **hotter** than those farther out, like **freezing** cold Neptune.

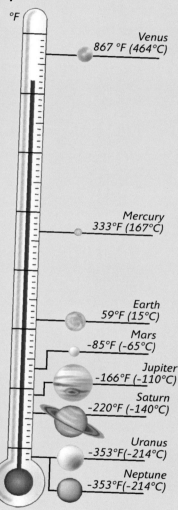

°F

Venus
867 °F (464°C)

Mercury
333°F (167°C)

Earth
59°F (15°C)

Mars
-85°F (-65°C)

Jupiter
-166°F (-110°C)

Saturn
-220°F (-140°C)

Uranus
-353°F(-214°C)

Neptune
-353°F(-214°C)

Tiny planets

In 2006, astronomers decided that Pluto is too small and its orbit is too unusual for it to be called a planet. They decided to call it a dwarf planet.

Another dwarf planet, called Eris, was discovered in 2005.

SUPER STAR

Our star, the Sun, is a giant ball of fiery, glowing gas. It provides the heat and light that sustains life on Earth. The Sun is vital to us, but it is only one of about 200 billion stars in our galaxy.

Sunspots are slightly cooler areas on the Sun's surface

Solar flares look like huge flames shooting out from the Sun's surface

zone

SALUTE THE SUN

Many ancient civilizations have worshipped the Sun. To the ancient Egyptians, the Sun god Ra was the king of the gods. They believed that he rode across the heavens in a boat every day, lighting up the sky. Ra was often shown with the head of a falcon and a Sun-shaped disc on his head.

TOTAL ECLIPSE

Sometimes the Sun, Moon, and Earth line up. As the Moon passes between the Sun and Earth, the Moon's shadow falls on Earth. This is called a solar eclipse. If you are in the darkest part of the shadow, you will see a total eclipse. In the partial shadow around this, you will see a partial eclipse.

The Moon passes in front of the Sun during a partial solar eclipse seen from China in May, 2012.

A solar prominence is a gigantic arc of hot hydrogen

The Sun is a giant fireball in space. Its dazzling surface is a boiling mass of glowing gas.

Eclipse kit

WARNING:
Never look at the Sun, especially with binoculars or a telescope. This can seriously damage your eyes or even make you blind.

To see how an eclipse works, you can make this model. You will need to ask an adult for help.

SUPPLIES

shoebox • scissors • black card stock • yellow tissue paper • sticky tape • toothpicks

HOW TO MAKE

1. Cut a window at each end of your shoebox and then cut a slit across the top of the box.

2. Cut out a square of black card stock small enough to slide into the slit in the box.

3. Cut a circle out of the middle of the card stock; stick yellow tissue paper over the hole.

4. Stick a toothpick to the black circle (you will use this as your Moon).

5. Slide the square of card stock into the slit in the box and hold the box up to the light. Look through it to see your Sun.

HOW TO USE
Push your Moon into the slit in the box behind the square of card stock. Move it slowly across your Sun to make an eclipse.

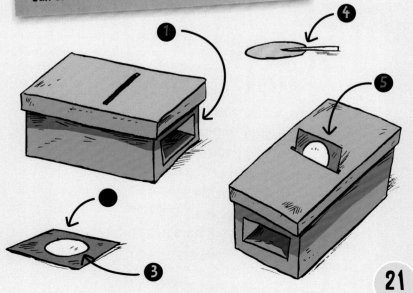

ROCKY WORLDS

The four planets closest to the Sun are smaller than the other four planets. They're made of rock and have few moons, or none at all. One of these planets is our home — Earth. We live on the third planet from the Sun.

Spewing volcanoes

All four rocky worlds have volcanoes, or had them in the past.

Mars has the biggest volcano in the solar system — Olympus Mons.

Venus has more volcanoes than any other planet in the solar system.

HOT STUFF

Mercury is the closest planet to the Sun, but Venus is the hottest planet. It is covered by a blanket of thick clouds that soak up lots of heat from the Sun like a giant greenhouse.

WHERE ARE ALL THE MARTIANS?

In the 1870s, astronomer Giovanni Schiaparelli looked through a telescope at Mars. He thought he saw straight lines on the planet. Astronomer Percival Lowell saw them, too. He thought they were canals built by Martians. However, the first spacecraft that visited Mars in the 1960s found no canals or Martians.

These four rocky worlds (not shown in order) are also known as the inner planets, because they are the closest planets to the Sun.

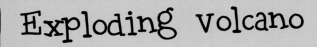

Exploding volcano

Volcanoes spew out molten rock called lava. You can make your own volcano and see this happening!

SUPPLIES

plastic sheet • earth or damp sand • small bottle • baking soda • dishwashing liquid • red and yellow food coloring • vinegar

HOW TO MAKE

1. On a plastic sheet, make your volcano out of earth or damp sand around a small bottle in the middle.

2. Add 3 tablespoons of baking soda and one tablespoon of dishwashing liquid to the bottle. Then add a few drops of each food coloring.

HOW TO USE

Pour some vinegar into the bottle and stand back. The vinegar and baking soda will react together, producing lots of carbon dioxide gas, which will make bubbles (helped by the soap), producing a foaming, frothing eruption. The food coloring will color your erupting lava.

GOLDILOCKS EARTH

Earth is a Goldilocks planet, which means it is not too far from the Sun or too close to it — it's just right for life. If Earth was closer to the Sun, it would be too hot for anything to live here, and if it was farther away it would be too cold.

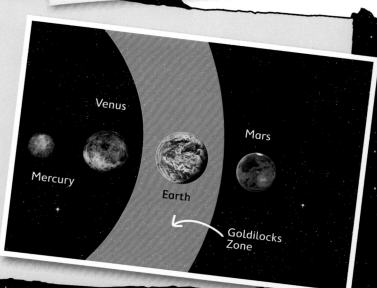

Mercury

Venus

Earth

Mars

Goldilocks Zone

GASSY GIANTS

The four planets farthest from the Sun are the biggest planets in the solar system. You can't land on them because they don't have any solid ground. These huge planets are mostly made of liquid and gas.

The four gas giants (not shown in order) are different colors because they have different chemicals in their clouds.

ICY RINGS

All four of the giant gas planets have rings around them. However, the rings around Jupiter, Uranus, and Neptune are thin, dusty, and dark, so they're hard to see. Saturn's rings are bright and easy to see because they're made of ice, which is good at reflecting sunlight.

GREAT RED SPOT

Look at any close-up photograph of Jupiter and the first thing you notice is a big red oval — this is the Great Red Spot. It's a giant storm that has been rolling around Jupiter for at least 300 years. The Great Red Spot is three times the size of Earth!

Speedy planets

Planets close to the Sun travel through space faster than planets farther away. You can see this with a paper planet.

SUPPLIES

newspaper • water-based paint
• string • stape

HOW TO MAKE

1. Make a planet from a ball of tightly scrunched-up newspaper. You could even paint your paper planet to look like a real planet — make it stripy like Jupiter or red like Mars.

2. Tie a three-foot-long piece of string around your paper planet and secure it with tape.

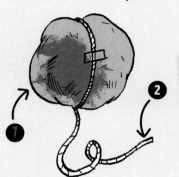

HOW TO USE

In an open space outside, hold the end of the string and swing your planet around above your head. The pull of the string acts like gravity and pulls the planet around into a circular orbit. Now hold the string in the middle. You'll find that you have to swing the planet around faster.

What a gas!

Uranus was the first planet to be discovered by someone using a telescope — William Herschel in **1781.**

Jupiter is made mostly of hydrogen, which stars are made of. If Jupiter had grown ten times bigger, it would have become a **star!**

LONG AND SLOW

The gas giants take a long time to go around the Sun. Jupiter takes nearly 12 years, Saturn takes 29 years, Uranus takes 84 years, and Neptune takes 165 years.

SPACE ROCKS

Planets and moons aren't the only things flying around the solar system. Countless smaller rocks swarm around the Sun, too. Most of them are too small and too far away for us to see, even with a telescope, but we know they're there.

Jupiter

Millions of pieces of rock swarm around the Sun in a broad belt between Mars and Jupiter.

Amazing asteroids!

The smallest asteroids are about the size of a house. The **biggest** are nearly **620 miles** (1,000 km) across!

Asteroid Ceres
Discovered 1801
**Diameter
591.5 miles**
(952 km)

Asteroid Pallas
Discovered 1802
**Diameter
591.5 miles**
(952 km)

Asteroid Vesta
Discovered 1807
**Diameter
326 miles**
(525 km)

Asteroid belt

FLYING APART

The pieces of rock orbiting the Sun in the asteroid belt might have joined together if it were not for Jupiter. Jupiter's gravity pulls the rocks apart. It also stops most of them from flying closer to the Sun and perhaps hitting Earth. Scientists keep an eye on all the big asteroids in case any of them head our way.

SHOOTING STARS

If you look up into a clear night sky, you might see a streak of light. It's called a meteor or shooting star, but it isn't a star. It's a tiny bit of rock from space flying into the air around Earth. It heats up until it glows and quickly burns up.

Shooting stars streak across the sky during a meteor shower.

This giant crater in Arizona was made by a meteorite.

Mars

Space rock hunt

Space rocks fall to Earth every day. They're called meteorites. Most of them are tiny and harmless. You can look for them with a magnet.

SUPPLIES

bucket or bowl • newspaper • magnet • small plastic bag • sheet of white paper • magnifying glass

WHAT TO DO

1. Put a bucket or bowl outside when it rains. If possible, put it under a drain spout from a roof to collect lots of water.

2. When it's full, take out any large twigs and leaves, and then carefully pour away most of the water. You should find some fine, dark, dusty dirt at the bottom.

3. Pour the last few drops of water with the dark particles onto a sheet of newspaper, and set the paper aside indoors until it dries out.

4. Put a magnet inside a small plastic bag and move it slowly back and forth across the paper. Some of the particles may stick to the outside of the bag.

5. Turn the bag inside out and take the magnet away. The dark dust is now inside the bag. Carefully empty the bag onto a sheet of white paper.

KNOBBLY WORLDS

Most asteroids and meteoroids have a knobbly shape. Their tiny pull of gravity isn't strong enough to pull them into a round shape like a planet. Craters on their surface show where other asteroids and meteoroids have crashed into them.

NO, TAKE THIS!

TAKE THAT!

HOW TO USE

Have a look at the particles through a magnifying glass. You've collected micrometeorites — tiny rocks from space. Sand, dust, and dirt don't stick to a magnet, but rocks from space do, because they contain iron.

27

COSMIC SNOWBALLS

If you look up into the sky one night and see something like a star with a long, bright tail, your eyes aren't playing tricks on you. You're looking at a comet — a mountain of ice and rock orbiting the Sun.

Astronomers saw a **comet** slamming into the planet **Jupiter** in 1994.

Gas tail

Dust tail

A big bright comet with long tails is a spectacular sight in the night sky. A comet's tails can be as long as **99 million miles** (160 million km).

TELLING TAILS

A comet's tails always point away from the Sun. Gas and dust around a comet's head are stretched out into tails by sunlight and a stream of particles given out by the Sun, called the solar wind — so the tails are always pushed away from the Sun.

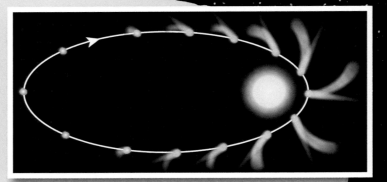

As a comet nears the Sun, its tails grow longer and brighter. When the comet passes the Sun and flies away from it, its tails fade.

ICE WORLDS

The solar system is surrounded by millions of comets. If you could travel past Neptune, you'd find a swarm of comets and icy worlds called the Kuiper Belt, which includes the dwarf planet Pluto. Even further away, there is another swarm of comets called the Oort Cloud.

BAD LUCK

In 1066, a comet appeared just as soldiers were gathering to fight the Battle of Hastings in England. When King Harold of England saw it, he thought it was a sign of bad luck. He then lost the battle!

Famous comets

Halley's Comet has been returning every 76 years for at least **2,250** years. Look out for it in **2061!**

In **1770**, Lexell's Comet came closer to **Earth** than any other comet. It looked as big as the **Moon**.

The brightest comet ever seen appeared in **1882**. It was brighter than the **Moon** and could be seen in daylight.

A tale of tails

A comet grows brighter the closer it is to the Sun. See this happening by making your own comet.

SUPPLIES

black card stock • scissors • colored pencils or crayons (black and yellow) • hole punch (or sharp pencil) • split pin

HOW TO USE

Hold the top card still and slowly turn the bottom sheet. You'll see your comet grow brighter as it comes closer to the Sun, with its tail pointing away from the Sun, just like a real comet.

HOW TO MAKE

1. Cut out a square of black card stock and draw an ellipse (a stretched circle) on it. Draw a bright yellow sun near one end of the ellipse.

2. Use the hole punch to make holes about one centimeter apart all along the line of your ellipse. Or you can push a sharp pencil through the card stock to make the holes. Make sure you can see through the holes.

3. Take another sheet of black card stock and cut out a circle bigger than the square. Draw a bright yellow strip from the center to the edge. Make the part near the center the brightest and then make the yellow color fade out towards the edge.

4. Place the card stock with the Sun on it on top of the other piece of card stock. Push a split pin through the Sun and the center of the other sheet to hold the two sheets together.

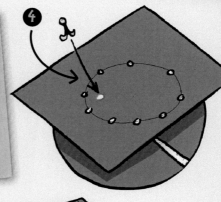

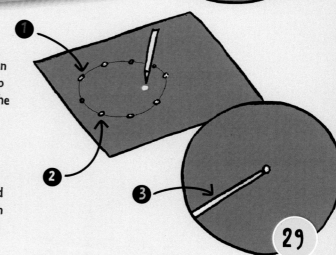

29

EXPLORING SPACE

Since the first spacecraft was launched in 1957, astronauts have landed on the Moon, robot spacecraft have explored the solar system, and telescopes have probed distant parts of the Universe. You might be able to explore space yourself in the future!

ROBOT EXPLORERS

The farthest that people have traveled from Earth is the Moon, but robot spacecraft have now flown past, orbited, or landed on every planet in the solar system. Some spacecraft have used their instruments to look far out into the rest of the universe.

The New Horizons space probe is on its way to the dwarf planet Pluto.

The biggest **spacecraft** ever built is the International Space Station. It's **so big** that it can be seen without a telescope. It looks like a **star**.

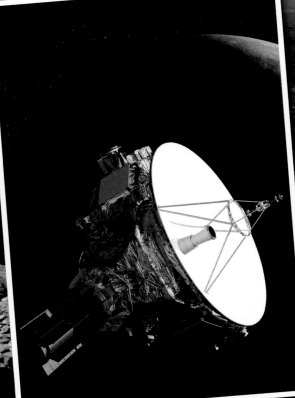

MARS ROVER

The Curiosity rover moves around Mars studying the surface and atmosphere. Its robot arm can reach out to take a closer look at interesting rocks. Curiosity is the fourth rover to be sent to Mars since 1996, and it's the biggest. Scientists decide where it should go and then send it instructions by radio.

Curiosity is a mobile science laboratory the size of a car that landed on Mars in 2012 to study the red planet.

Balloon rocket

The rockets that launch spacecraft power themselves into space on a jet of gas. Make a balloon rocket to see how this works.

SUPPLIES

string • drinking straw • long balloon • tape

HOW TO MAKE

1. Tie one end of the string to something solid and secure, like a doorknob.

2. Thread the string through the drinking straw and tie the other end to something solid and secure several feet away, so that the string is tight.

3. Blow up the balloon and, while holding the neck, stick the balloon to the drinking straw with the tape.

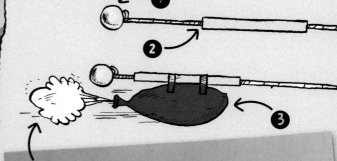

HOW TO USE

Let go of the balloon and watch it fly along the string. The air escaping from the balloon pushes it along, like the fiery jet of burning gas from a rocket. The pushing force that moves the balloon and a real rocket is called thrust.

SPACE TELESCOPES

Most telescopes are built on top of mountains, where they are above most of Earth's atmosphere. In the clear, thin air above the clouds, they get a better view of space. Some telescopes go even further — they've been launched into orbit around Earth to get an even clearer view!

This image of the Helix Nebula was taken from the Spitzer Space Telescope, launched from Cape Canaveral in Florida in 2003.

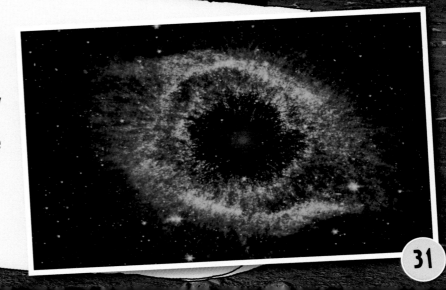

INDEX

ACKNOWLEDGMENTS

The publishers would like to thank the following artists who have contributed to this book:
Cover: Rob McClurkan (The Bright Agency)
Insides: Peter Bull, Sarah Horne (Advocate Art) and Stuart Jackson-Carter

All other artwork from the Miles Kelly Artwork Bank

The publishers would like to thank the following sources for the use of their photographs:
t = top, b = bottom, l = left, r = right, c = center, bg = background, rt = repeated throughout

NASA 11 NASA, H. Fort (JHU), G. Illingworth (USCS/LO), M. Clampin (STScI), G. Hartig (STScI), the ACS Science Team, and ESA; 12–13 NASA, ESA, and M. Livio and the Hubble 20th Anniversary Team (STScI); 12 NASA, ESA and The Hubble Heritage Team (STScI/AURA); 13 NASA, ESA, J. Hester, A. Loll (ASU), Andrew Fruchter; 16(t) NASA/MOLA Science Team/ O. de Goursac, Adrian Lark, (c) NASA, JHU APL, CIW, (b) NASA/JPL; 17 NASA Jet Propulsion Laboratory (NASA-JPL); 18; 19(t) NASA/JPL, (c), (b) Thierry Lombry/NASA; 30–31 NASA/JPL-Caltech; 31 JPL-Caltech, Kate Su (Steward Obs, U. Arizona) et al.

Rex 21 KeystoneUSA-ZUMA

Science Photo Library 4–5 Babak Tafreshi, Twan; 6–7 Jose Antonio Peñas; 8 Jose Antonio Peñas; 14–15 Mark Garlick; 16–19 Detlev Van Ravenswaay; 20–21 Henning Dalhoff; 27 Walter Pacholka, Astropics; 30 NASA; 31 NASA

Shutterstock 4(br/rt) tanatat; 5 Rafael Pacheco; 15 John A Davis; 16(postcard rt) Irena Misevic

Every effort has been made to acknowledge the source and copyright holder of each picture. Miles Kelly Publishing apologises for any unintentional errors or omissions.